KiDS' LETTERS to
★ President ★
BUSH

Compiled and edited by Bill Adler

Illustrations by Chuck Rekow

RUTLEDGE HILL PRESS

Nashville, Tennessee

A Division of Thomas Nelson Publishers

Since 1798

www.thomasnelson.com

Published by Rutledge Hill Press, a Division of Thomas Nelson, Inc., P.O. Box 141000,
Nashville, Tennessee 37214.

Ruthedge Hill Press books may be purchased in bulk for educational, business,
fundraising, or sales promotional use. For information, please e-mail
SpecialMarkets@ThomasNelson.com.

Library of Congress Cataloging-in-Publication Data

Kids' letters to President Bush / edited by Bill Adler ; illustrations by Chuck Rekow.
p. cm.
ISBN 1-4016-0204-5 (hardcover)
1. Bush, George W. (George Walker), 1946-—Correspondence.
2. Children—United States—Correspondence. 3. American letters. 4. Children's writings,
American. 5. Bush, George W. (George Walker), 1946——Humor.
6. American wit and humor. I. Adler, Bill, 1929- II. Rekow, Chuck.
E903.A4 2005
973.931'092—dc22
2004022814

Printed in the United States of America

05 06 07 08 09 — 5 4 3 2 1

To all the young Americans
who wrote to the president and expressed
their dreams and opinions

Foreword

In 1962 I edited a book titled *Kids' Letters to President Kennedy.* The response to the book was phenomenal and the book became a national bestseller. It was obvious that Americans, young and old, enjoyed reading the letters that young people wrote to the president of the United States.

Since *Kids' Letters to President Kennedy* was published, we have published collections of *Kids' Letters to President Johnson, President Carter,* and *President Reagan.*

The book that you are now reading contains letters from young people all over the country to President Bush. Teachers from hundreds of schools encouraged their students to write to the president and then shared those letters with us. The most exciting experience the children had was getting letters back from the White

House and realizing that our president wants to hear from all of America's citizens.

Nothing expresses the sentiments of young people better than their letters. We hope you enjoy reading this book as much as we enjoyed putting it together.

I am most grateful to Jan Crozier for her assistance in making this book a reality.

Dear President Bush,

My uncle bet $5 that you would win the election.

Does he have to pay taxes on the $5?

Your friend,
Christopher P., AGE 11
Amarillo, TX

Dear President Bush,

Maybe your brother Jeb will be president.

My brother will never be president because he is stupid and doesn't like to read.

Love,
Betsy W., AGE 8
Newark, NJ

Dear Mr. President,

How much money does a president make?

Could you please write and tell me because if it isn't enough money then I will be a dentist.

Timothy U., AGE 7
Jamestown, NY

Dear Mr. President,

What do you do for fun?

Do you have play dates with the vice president?

Gary D., AGE 7

Kingman, AZ

Dear Mr. President,

Me and my grandpa saw the funeral of President Reagan on TV.

My grandpa would like to be buried the same way.

Lisa P., AGE 9

Dayton, OH

Dear President Bush,

Do you play golf? I read in a newspaper that every president liked to play golf.

Maybe Tiger Woods should be a president.

Kyle P., AGE 10

Long Beach, CA

Dear Mr. President,

Did you ever see a *Harry Potter* movie?

They are exciting and the good side always wins. Maybe you could show the movies to the army so they can win the war in Iraq and come home soon.

Matthew C., AGE 10
Wilmington, DE

Dear President Bush,

The worst thing about being president is that nobody leaves you alone. Maybe you could hide at Camp David.

John J., AGE 7
Lincoln, NE

Dear Mr. Bush,

Where does the First Lady buy her clothes? She always looks beautiful. My mom looks beautiful too and she buys her clothes at K-Mart and Target.

Victoria C., AGE 8
Bend, OR

Dear President Bush,

When will we have a woman president?
I am ready.

Brooke A., AGE 10
Peoria, IL

Dear Mr. President,

I have never been to Washington but I have been to Disneyland.

Is Washington as much fun as Disneyland?
Samantha P., AGE 8
Valdosta, GA

Dear Mr. President,

Do you know how to play chess? I am the best chess player in my school and I would like to come to the White House to play chess with you.

I promise I won't beat you.

Dylan C., AGE 13
Spokane, WA

Dear Mr. President,

Do you drink milk?

It is very important that you drink three glasses of milk every day. My father told me that and he is a doctor.

Your friend,
Eric K., AGE 8
Chicago, IL

P.S. He could come to the White House and give you a free checkup.

Dear President Bush,

I read in the newspaper that you go fishing with your father.

I go fishing with my father but he isn't president of anything. We don't catch many fish either.

Connor M., AGE 8
Portland, OR

Dear Mr. President,

If I were president I would make a law that says you can't yell at kids.

Thank you,
Noah N., AGE 8
Humboldt, TN

Dear Mr. President,

Do you get mad when they don't say nice things about you on TV?

Maybe you should just watch the weather reports.

Nancy D., AGE 9
Cincinnati, OH

Dear President Bush,

Please send me an autographed picture.

Please write on the picture "To my good friend Lisa. Love, the President."

Nobody will know it's not true except you and me.

> *Lisa D.,* AGE 10
> Boise, ID

Dear President Bush,

Do you know all the words to "The Star Spangled Banner"?

If you don't I could come to the White House and teach you the words.

> Your friend,
> *Bobby K.,* AGE 8
> Seattle, WA

P.S. I won't charge you.

Dear President Bush,

I think you are the best president since Lincoln.

Lincoln was a great president because he freed the slaves but not the kids.

Your friend,
Trisha K., AGE 8
Queens, NY

Dear President Bush,

Do you get free clothes when you are president?

My uncle says that the president gets everything for free, even his toothpaste.

Love,
Nicole H., AGE 7
Seattle, WA

Dear President Bush,

I am glad you won the election.

I knew you would win because all the girls in my class thought you were cute.

Marcella V., AGE 7
Carlsbad, NM

Dear President Bush,

What do you like best about being the president?

I think the thing I would like best about being president would be getting letters from smart girls like me.

> Love,
> *Maria H.,* AGE 11
> San Diego, CA

Dear Mr. President,

I read that you have your own swimming pool and movie theater in the White House.

That is real cool. The only cool thing we have in our house is a dishwasher.

> *Ellen S.,* AGE 8
> Charlotte, NC

Dear President Bush,

Were you surprised when you won the election? Too bad you didn't bet that you would win.

> *Mark P.,* AGE 10
> Bridgeport, CT

Dear President Bush,

Do you have any friends in Congress?

My mom says your only friend is the vice president.

Richard D., AGE **8**
Greenwich, CT

Dear Mr. President,

Someday there will be a woman who will be president.

I hope so because women are smart, especially my mom.

Jessica D., AGE **10**
Rockport, ME

Dear Mr. Bush,

Did you ever tell a lie?

George Washington never told a lie, but I'm not sure about the other presidents.

Your friend,
Joshua, AGE 7
Minneapolis, MN

Dear President Bush,

    If we sent soldiers to Iraq because they were supposed to have weapons of mass destruction there and we didn't find them, why didn't we just come home and say it was a mistake?

    My mom said I should never be embarrassed to say I made a mistake.

Sidney J.

Age 10

Alexandria, VA

Dear President Bush,

Do you think we will have another war? I hope not.

My grandfather was in World War II and he told me it wasn't fun.

Scott C., AGE 9
Phoenix, AZ

Dear Mr. President,

When did you ask the First Lady to marry you?

Did she say yes because she knew you would be president and she wanted to be First Lady?

John D., AGE 11
Miami, FL

Dear President Bush,

Is Congress smart? Please write me your answer.

Thank you,
Megan L., AGE 8
Lake Tahoe, CA

P.S. I promise not to tell anyone.

Dear President Bush,

Do your friends have a nickname for you? They used to call President Reagan "the Gipper."

What would you like to be called? How about "the Chief"?

Jeffrey H., AGE 9
Oklahoma City, OK

Dear President Bush,

Someday I hope there will be a woman president.

But not my sister. She will drive everybody crazy—the Democrats and Republicans.

A citizen,
Lawrence K., AGE 8
Atlanta, GA

Dear Mr. President,

When did you know you wanted to be president? Was it when you were a kid?

I am seven and I know that I want to be president or the pitcher for the New York Yankees.

Justin, AGE 7
Bronx, NY

Dear President Bush,

I think you are cute.

Do you know Dan Rather?

Could you please get me his autograph even if you have to say something nice about him to get the autograph?

Heather P., AGE 9
Kansas City, KS

P.S. My mom loves Dan Rather.

Dear Mr. Bush,

I think you are the smartest man in the whole world.

Could I come over to the White House so you can help me with my homework? I promise to vote for you when I grow up.

Matthew J., AGE 8
Cleveland, OH

Dear Sir,

Does your wife call you Mr. President?
My mom calls my father a lot of things.

> Your friend,
> *Patricia R.,* AGE 9
> Fargo, ND

Dear Mr. President,

I would like to join the army.

I would be a good soldier because I'm not afraid of anything except my big brother.

> *William B.,* AGE 8
> Nashville, TN

Dear President Bush,

Do you know Donald Trump? He is very famous and he is very rich.

Maybe he could lend money to our country, if we need extra money for schools or airports.

> *Jennifer K.,* AGE 9
> Fort Worth, TX

Dear Mr. President,

I would like to be the ambassador to China. I think I would be very good because I like Chinese food a lot.

Alex H., AGE 8
Charlotte, NC

Dear Mr. President,

What is your favorite book?

My mom said it is the Bible because you have to pray a lot.

Kimberly W., AGE 8
Meriden, CT

Dear Mr. Bush,

I hope we win the war in Iraq so all the soldiers can come home and go to Disneyland.

Eric M., AGE 6
Duluth, MN

Dear Mr. President,

Do you know any really famous people like movie stars or baseball stars or football stars or do you just know congressmen, senators and other people that think they are famous but really aren't?

Your friend,
Melissa H., AGE 11
Atlanta, GA

Dear Mr. President,

Do you have your own bathroom at the White House? That is why I want to be president.

There are six kids in my family and I can never get to use the bathroom unless I sit in front of the bathroom door before somebody gets there before me.

John S., AGE 7
Toledo, OH

Dear President Bush,

There are too many cats and dogs in Chicago. There are more cats and dogs than people. I like cats and dogs, but I like people better. Please help the people.

Ashley L., AGE 7
Chicago, IL

Dear President Bush,

I saw you on TV with your dog. He was very cute. Is your dog the president of other dogs?

Your citizen,
Amy T., AGE 9
Buffalo, NY

Dear President Bush,

I read that you like to play golf. Could I be your caddy?

I am very strong and I don't talk too much.

Justin T., AGE 10
Fort Lauderdale, FL

Dear Mr. President,

I hope we never have a war again.

Nobody likes war. Not even Michael who is the bully on my block.

Daniel N., AGE 7
Memphis, TN

Dear Mr. President,

I read in the newspaper that you like to play golf.

I hope you are a good golf player so you can make money as a golf pro when you leave the White House.

Daniel Z., AGE 11
Selma, AL

Dear Mr. President,

I would like to join the army when I am 18.

My mom wants me to go to college, but I want to join the army first so I can be a war hero when I go to college.

Michael, AGE 7
Hannibal, MO

Dear President Bush,

I am glad you are the president. I hope you are the president for a long time until I am ready to take your place as president, if my mother will let me.

Fred R., AGE 7
Baltimore, MD

Dear President Bush,

Can you help with the weather in Seattle?

It rains too much. My mom said not even the president can do anything about the weather. I hope she is wrong. We need more sunshine in Seattle.

Elizabeth P., AGE 8
Seattle, WA

Dear President Bush,

Please ask Congress to make a law that kids can watch six hours of TV a day.

My mom only lets me watch TV once a week. It is no fun and I promise to vote for you when I am 18 if you are still the president.

David M., AGE 7
San Francisco, CA

Dear Mr. President,

I don't know who you told about the Secret Service but everybody knows about it.

I never tell my little brother anything because he can't keep secrets.

Do you think you should call them something else because they are not a secret anymore?

Your friend,

Zachary S.

Age 9

Idaho Falls, ID

Dear President Bush,

Who makes more money—you or Derek Jeter?

I guess you make more money even if you can't hit or catch so good.

Tyler S., AGE 7
New York, NY

Dear President Bush,

If I were president I would only let girls go to my school.

Boys are dumb and they make too much noise.

Your citizen,
Paige D., AGE 7
Stockton, CA

Dear Mr. President,

I hope we never have to use the atomic bomb.

If we use the atomic bomb then there will be nobody left in the world except cats and dogs and fish.

Amanda F., AGE 9
Scranton, PA

Dear Mr. President,

Do you write your own speeches or does the First Lady write them for you?

Jamie L., AGE 9
Brookeville, MD

Dear Mr. Bush,

What does Congress do all day?

My dad told me that Congress doesn't do anything but make trouble.

Ralph N., AGE 8
Palm Beach, FL

Dear Mr. President,

I think you are cool. That is why you won the election.

The other candidate wasn't cool and that's why he lost.

Mark R., AGE 9
Sandusky, OH

Dear President Bush,

I hope you write a book when you are ex-president so everybody will know what you did for eight years.

My older sister and my Uncle Max argue a lot about whether you are working hard. My sister said you took a lot of vacations.

Richie K., AGE 9
Des Moines, IA

Dear President Bush,

Could you please come to my school and give a speech? Nobody interesting ever comes to my school except the mayor and nobody really listens to him.

Ella C., AGE 9
Long Beach, CA

Dear Mr. Bush,

I would like to come to the White House and tell you a funny story that will make you laugh.

I think a president needs to hear a good story so he can laugh more.

Angela M., AGE 8
Ann Arbor, MI

Dear Mr. President,

I thought Ronald Reagan was a great president.

He was very smart. My grandfather voted for him and he told me that he used to be an actor but he became president because he never won an Academy Award.

Zachary K., AGE **10**
Omaha, NE

Dear President Bush,

I liked your speech at the convention. You were very good.

Could you please send me a copy of your speech so I can use it when I run for class president of the fifth grade?

Thank you,
Brooke L., AGE **11**
Akron, OH

P.S. I will give you credit for the speech.

Dear President Bush,

I heard on TV that you have your own movie theater in the White House.

Do you also have a popcorn machine?

Brittany E., AGE 8
Savannah, GA

Dear Mr. President,

Could you please pass a law that says kids can't be spanked unless it is an emergency?

David R., AGE 7
Medina, OH

Dear President Bush,

What is the best thing about being president?

Is it the free plane, or the free house, or the free tickets for the football games?

Does a president pay for anything?

Nathan C., AGE 9
Brooklyn, NY

Dear Mr. President,

My grandmother is very sick but she can't pay for all her medicine.

Could you please send her $12 so she can get better? I love her a lot.

Lisa C., AGE 7
Little Rock, AR

Dear President Bush,

I would like you to speak at my school when I graduate.

I would like you to talk for three minutes.

I am sending you a picture and the story of my life so far.

Samantha, AGE 10
Johnstown, PA

Dear Mr. President,

What is your favorite sport?

My favorite sport is watching TV.

Your friend,
Arnie J., AGE 8
St. Louis, MO

Dear Mr. President,

You should go on more vacations.

Maybe you would like to go with me and my parents. We are going to Yellowstone Park for a week.

Tracy G., AGE 9
Milwaukee, WI

Dear President Bush,

Does the United States have a lot of enemies?

I would like to be a spy for our country so I can help you catch all the enemies of our country. You don't have to pay me.

I'll do it because I am a good American and I think it would be fun.

Richard R., AGE **10**
Portland, OR

Dear President Bush,

Do you pay for your own clothes or does the country pay for your clothes?

If the country pays for your clothes you should get them at the Gap because they are cheaper there and you could save the country a lot of money.

Linda H., AGE **10**
Stowe, VT

Dear Mr. President,

How old do you have to be to be in the army?

I am only eight, but I would like to be in the army before my next history test on Tuesday.

Michael G., AGE 8
Cheyenne, WY

Dear President Bush,

I think you should get your own TV station.

If they say something about you on the news that you don't like, you can use your own TV station to tell the truth.

Your friend,
Gregory P., AGE 9
LaGrange, GA

Dear Mr. President,

Do your kids like living in the White House?

If they don't like living in the White House they can live with us. We have an extra bedroom, a big yard and three bathrooms.

Ashley C., AGE 9
Memphis, TN

Dear Mr. President,

What will you do if the First Lady wants to be president next?

Will you help her become president or will you tell her no?

Mallory R., AGE 10
San Bernardino, CA

Dear President Bush,

I like you but I don't know why.

My father likes you but my mother doesn't.

My mother doesn't like anything my father likes.

Victoria L., AGE 7
Elizabeth, NJ

President Bush,

What would you do if you weren't the president?

Do you think you could get a good job?

Hunter J., AGE 7
Greensboro, NC

Dear President Bush,

Do you ever get to drive your own car or does the Secret Service always get to drive?

I'll bet when the Secret Service drives you never get a ticket for speeding.

My dad gets a lot of tickets for speeding.

Brett L., AGE 7
Scarsdale, NY

Dear Mr. President,

We need some more money for our school library.

The library is so poor that the last book we have about an American president is about President Lincoln.

Can you help us?

Joseph B., AGE 8
Brunswick, ME

Dear Mr. President,

You should smile more so everybody will think you are having fun as president even if you are not.

Christina K., AGE 9
Corpus Christi, TX

Dear Mr. President,

All the kids in my school like you and are glad you are the president except one kid.

But nobody likes him.

Jeremy J., AGE 7
Farmington, NM

Dear President Bush,

Do you have to be good-looking to be president?

I hope not because my best friend Raymond wants to be president when he grows up and I think he is kind of ugly.

Zachary B., AGE 8
Augusta, GA

Dear President Bush,

There is a lot of crime in my city.

There are too many crooks and they are all in my class.

Barry M., AGE 7
Bronx, NY

Dear President Bush,

Why do we always have so many wars in faraway places like Korea and Vietnam and Iraq?

I hope the wars stop soon because when I grow up I want to play hockey, not be a soldier.

Tyler M., AGE 10
Casa Grande, AZ

Dear President Bush,

I think that the First Lady is cute.

Is it okay for a kid to say that the First Lady is cute?

Joshua M., AGE 7
San Diego, CA

Dear Mr. President,

You are the best president since I was born. I am seven.

Lauren H., AGE 7
Carlsbad, NM

Dear President Bush,

My mom and dad told me if I get an A on my report card someday I might be president.

Was there ever a president who didn't get an A on their report card?

Please write and tell me.

Dennis G., AGE 7
Boston, MA

Dear President Bush,

I like your speeches. My mother likes your speeches. My Aunt Martha likes your speeches but my Uncle Stanley falls asleep.

Your friend,
Martin F., AGE 8
Manchester, NH

Dear Mr. President,

I would like to get federal assistance to help clean up my room.

My mother always says it is too messy but I can't clean up my room by myself.

Can you help?

Brian R.

Age 9

Dayton, OH

Dear President Bush,

Do you go to church on Sunday?

I hope you do because my mother says our country needs all the help we can get from God.

Melissa, AGE **9**
La Fayette, IN

Dear President Bush,

I don't think it is right that Madonna makes more money than the president.

Maybe you should learn to sing.

Erica G., AGE **8**
Kimball, NE

Dear President Bush,

How many TV sets do you have in the White House?

Is it fun to see yourself on TV?

I think you are very handsome on TV even when you are mad.

Alice G., AGE **9**
Americus, GA

Dear Mr. President,

My friend Sammy told me the vice president said a bad word to somebody.

Did the FBI yell at him or send him to his room?

Eric P., AGE 8
Bronx, NY

Dear Mr. President,

We need the FBI right away.

Somebody is stealing the candy bars from the vending machines at school. Thank you,

Austin H., AGE 7
Houston, TX

Dear Mr. President,

My father is a good citizen but he doesn't have enough money to pay his taxes.

Could you lend him the money?

I promise he will pay you back.

Heather T., AGE 8
Glendale, RI

Dear President Bush,
Roses are red.
Violets are blue.
You are the best president
I ever knew.

Rachel E., AGE **8**
Binghamton, NM

Dear Mr. President,

Do you have many picnics on the White House lawn?

My mom makes really good fried chicken and if you invited us I bet she would make enough for you and the First Lady.

We could play basketball if you have a basketball hoop, or play catch on the lawn.

Benjamin D., AGE **8**
Myrtle Beach, SC

Dear Mr. President,

I hope I can be president someday but my mother says first I should get a real job and work.

Jerome F., AGE 7
New York, NY

Dear Mr. President,

My favorite restaurant is McDonald's. Does the Secret Service let you eat there?

Harry M., AGE 9
Phoenix, AZ

Dear President Bush,

I would like to come to the White House and sleep in the White House.

I never slept in a president's house before. I promise to make the bed in the morning. And I never wet the bed.

Brandon H., AGE 7
Baton Rouge, LA

Dear Mr. President,

Is Saddam Hussein the meanest man in the world?

I bet Tony who is the meanest kid in our school could beat him up.

Albert P., AGE 9
Los Angeles, CA

Dear President Bush,

What time do you get up in the morning?
Do you get up before 9:00 a.m.?

I like to sleep late so I won't run for president even if I could win.

Todd H., AGE 9
Milford, DE

Dear President Bush,

I hope you will be the president for a long time.

I am only eight but I would like to vote for you someday.

Cynthia G., AGE 8
Clayville, RI

Dear President Bush,

I saw on TV that the Red Cross was helping people clean up after a tornado.

Could they come help me because it's my turn to clean up our yard and the garage?

Paul G., AGE 10
Buffalo, NY

Dear President Bush,

Where did you meet the First Lady?

My mom and dad met at the bowling alley and my dad wanted to marry her right away because she beat him at bowling.

Sharon T., AGE 9
Danville, IL

Dear Mr. Bush,

I would like to bring my dog Ruff to visit you at the White House.

He is a very good dog and he is trained so he won't mess up the White House and he doesn't bark much and he doesn't bite at all.

He sleeps most of the time and he is a very good watchdog.

Glen C., AGE 8
Columbus, IN

Dear President Bush,

How much money does the First Lady make?

I hope she makes a lot because without the First Lady you would have to clean the White House or wash the dishes.

Kristin W., AGE 9
Bridgeport, CT

Dear Mr. Bush,

I think you won the election because you were a better speaker even if a lot of people didn't know what you were talking about.

Tracey O., AGE 10
Green Valley, AZ

Dear President Bush,

What does the vice president do all day?

I have asked a lot of grownups and nobody knows the answer.

Shannon D., AGE 8
Bismarck, ND

Dear Mr. President,

My dad said you don't have friends in Congress.
Maybe you should have a party or a picnic at the
White House so you can make more friends.

Rachel C., AGE **8**
Manchester, CT

Dear President Bush,

I would like a picture of you when you were a
kid. It doesn't have to be a good picture.

Michael P., AGE 7
Athens, GA

P.S. I will send you a picture of me when I was
younger.

Dear Mr. President,

Is God an American? Please write me if you
know the answer.

Wendy W., AGE **8**
Bardstown, KY

Dear President Bush,

My mother voted for you.

My father voted for you.

My Uncle John voted for you.

My Aunt Alice didn't vote for you but she doesn't like anybody except Clint Eastwood.

Stephanie S., AGE 8
Cranston, RI

Dear President Bush,

You should try to get on the *American Idol* program.

That will make you really famous and all the kids in the world will know who you are. Even if you can't sing too good they might take you on the program.

Whitney C., AGE 9
Burlington, VT

Dear President Bush,

Who is the boss in the White House? You or the FBI?

Your citizen,
Judy L., AGE 6
Brooklyn, NY

Dear Mr. President,

I don't have any money.

Could you please send me $5 from the U.S. Treasury?

I don't think anybody will know that the $5 is missing.

Zach S., AGE 7
Middletown, DE

Dear President Bush,

I think you were very good during the campaign debates.

My father only fell asleep three times.

Tracey F., AGE 10
Davenport, IA

Dear Mr. President,

Do you have a cat at the White House?

My cat Cindy just had four kittens and I would like to give you and the First Lady a kitten. Her name is Patty. Patty is very cute and she won't scratch the furniture at the White House.

Heather L., AGE 7
Athens, SD

Dear President Bush,

There are a lot of people who drive their cars too fast in St. Louis.

I think there should be a law that you can never drive more than 10 miles an hour even if you are in a hurry.

Michael T., AGE 8
St. Louis, MO

Dear President Bush,

I read in the newspapers that the First Lady is a very good cook.

My mom used to be a good cook but now she only orders take-out food.

I hope the First Lady never does that to you.

Sarah P.

Age 10

Atlantic City, NJ

Dear Mr. Bush,

Do you know President Clinton?
He was a good talker just like you.

Rachel B., AGE 11
Des Moines, IA

Dear President Bush,

Did you always want to be president?

I am seven and I don't know what I want to be except I don't want to be a doctor because I am afraid of needles.

Justin K., AGE 7
Auburn, AL

Dear President Bush,

Could you please pass a law so kids don't have to do more than one hour of homework at night?

I never have time to watch TV now.

Brandon R., AGE 9
Clovis, NM

Dear Mr. President,

I would like my birthday to be a national holiday. My birthday is May 14th.

You can call the holiday "Bobby's Day."

Your friend,
Bobby R., AGE 9
St. Louis, MO

Dear Mr. Bush,

How much money does a president make in an hour?

I would like to know because I only get 75 cents and I have to mow our lawn.

Are there any laws about how much kids should get paid?

Thank you,
Christopher E., AGE 9
Harrisburg, PA

Dear President Bush,
Who is the boss in your house?
You or the First Lady or the Secret Service?
Ellen S., AGE 7
Americus, GA

Dear Mr. President,
I am nine years old and I would like to be president so my girlfriend Susan can be the First Lady.
Susan would be a great First Lady. She is very smart and she doesn't talk too much.
Albert B., AGE 9
West Point, NY

Dear President Bush,
Would you rather be a king than a president?
Maybe you could be the first king in this country.
Brett B., AGE 7
Madison, WI

Dear President Bush,

Here are the names of the bad kids in my school.

> Mark
> Larry
> Steve
> Billy
> Freddy
> Bruce

Please have them arrested.
They are all my best friends sometimes.

Michael C., AGE 7
Exeter, RI

Dear Mr. President,

I think you should let me be the ambassador to the United Nations so I can tell the whole world how great America is.

They will believe me because I am like George Washington. I never tell lies.

Emma W., AGE 9
Modesto, CA

Dear President Bush,

Could you please fix the traffic light in front of our house?

It doesn't work right and I have to wait too long to cross the street with my bike.

Ethan W., AGE 7
Biloxi, MS

Dear Mr. President,

I like your speeches a lot except when they are boring or too long.

Gregory M., AGE 8
Austin, TX

Dear President Bush,

My girlfriend Betsy and me would like to get married in the White House when we get married someday.

We will be married in 20 years.

Peter N., AGE 7
Bismarck, ND

Dear President Bush,

I would like to fly on Air Force One so I could visit my cousin in Omaha.

I don't have enough money to buy a ticket on a real plane.

Melissa B., AGE 8
Barrington, RI

Dear President Bush,

Did you know you wanted to be president when you were in the first grade?

I am in the first grade and I don't know what I want to be when I grow up.

I will decide when I am in the third grade.

Matthew R., AGE 6
Auburn, AL

Dear Mr. President,

I think you should smile more.

Aren't you having any fun being president?

Marlene K., AGE 6
Hastings, NE

Dear President Bush,

Did you ever want to be a policeman or a fireman? I think policemen and firemen look handsome in their uniforms.

Do you think a president or a vice president should have uniforms?

Maybe they could look like Spiderman—that would be cool.

Megan B., AGE 9
Fresno, CA

Dear Mr. Bush,

Do you have a nickname?

I read in my history book that everybody called President Eisenhower "Ike" and President Roosevelt "FDR" and President Kennedy "JFK."

Maybe they could call you the "big boss."

Michelle Y., AGE 8
Cedar Rapids, IA

Dear President Bush,

I hope we don't have any more trouble in Iraq.

I am eight and I don't want to have to go in the army when I am eighteen to fight in Iraq.

My mother wouldn't let me go.

Richard C., AGE 8
Clovis, NM

Dear President Bush,

I would like to be president when I grow up but first I would like to be a millionaire like Bill Gates.

Mark M., AGE 7
Florence, SC

Dear President Bush,

What will you do when you become the ex-president?

Is it hard for an ex-president to get a job? Maybe you could be a school crossing guard at our school.

Brett J., AGE 8
Fremont, NE

Dear Mr. President,

It costs a lot to eat lunch at my school.

We need a million dollars so the school can give us hot dogs or pizza every day for lunch.

Thank you,
Amy J., AGE 9
Brookeville, MD

Dear President Bush,

My dad says the best thing about being president is that you don't have to carry out the garbage or dry the dishes.

Martin P., AGE 9
Alamogordo, NM

Dear Mr. President,

I would like to be the first woman president.
I am very smart and I am a good cook too.

Angela M., AGE 9
Omaha, NE

Dear President Bush,

My father is too fat.

My mom tries to get him to lose weight but he keeps eating pizza.

Could you please write to my father to tell him to stop eating pizza or you will put him in jail?

Brian D., AGE 7
New Haven, CT

Dear Mr. President,

When I grow up I want to be the vice president.

I don't think the vice president does anything except talk on TV.

It is a great job.

Jimmy D., AGE 9
Athens, AL

Dear Mr. President,

I think our books in school should have more pictures so kids will want to study more.

Your friend,
Lisa W., AGE 8
Queens, NY

P.S. Please don't tell my teacher I sent this letter.

Dear Mr. President,

What does the First Lady do all day?

My mom works in an office because she hates to clean the house.

Does the First Lady clean the White House? Please write.

Grace D., AGE 9
Jefferson City, TN

Dear Mr. President,

Are you a good football player?

Our team at school hasn't won any games this year and we really need some good players.

If you aren't a good football player, how about the vice president?

Nicholas M., AGE 11
Oklahoma City, OK

Dear President Bush,

I don't think we should be in Iraq and other foreign places.

We have enough problems in Atlanta.

Amy L., AGE **8**
Atlanta, GA

Dear Mr. President,

Did you ever get into trouble when you were a boy?

I am nine and I have gotten into a lot of trouble and I hope it doesn't keep me from being president someday.

Timothy J., AGE **9**
North Platte, NE

Dear President Bush,

I think you are very handsome and I would like to meet you someday when you are not too busy with the Congress. My friends say I am very cute.

Love,
Amanda A., AGE **9**
Hastings, NC

Dear President Bush,

If you have a vice president, does the First Lady have a second lady?

Erin M., AGE 9
Chandler, AZ

Dear President Bush,

If I were president I would give everybody in the country $10 for their birthday. My birthday is September 10th.

Love,
Susan K., AGE 8
Albany, NY

Dear Mr. President,

Why does a baseball player make more money than the president?

Maybe you should play baseball.

Your friend,
Ralph S., AGE 8
Newark, NJ

P.S. You could play third base on our Little League team.

Dear President Bush,

I would like to visit Camp David next summer.

The camp that I go to is very boring and I think Camp David would be more fun.

I can come on July 4th.

James P.

Age 9

Portland, ME

Dear Mr. President,

Do you have to work seven days a week when you are president?

I would like to be president someday but not if you have to work too hard.

Nicholas S., AGE 9
Gadsden, AL

Dear Mr. President,

I think you could save a lot of money for the country if we only had school every other week.

Jason, AGE 7
Clayville, RI

Dear President Bush,

Please fix our taxes. My dad doesn't have enough money left for my allowance.

Thank you,
Sterling L., AGE 8
Boise, ID

Dear President Bush,

Even though they can't vote, you should do more for cats and dogs.

Love,
Gloria G., AGE 7
Akron, OH

Dear Mr. President,

Did you ever tell a lie?

My father says that presidents never tell a lie unless they are in big trouble.

Is the war in Iraq big trouble?

Michael C., AGE 8
Shreveport, LA

Dear President Bush,

I think gas prices are too high.

If you don't do something, everybody will have to ride bicycles or roller-skate. I don't think my grandmother can learn to roller-skate.

Your pal,
Steve P., AGE 9
San Francisco, CA

Dear President of the United States,

I am glad you won the election.

My mom and dad voted for you and are glad you won the election.

My Aunt Millie was very upset.

Gail N., AGE 7
Greene, RI

Dear Mr. President,

What will you do on vacation?

Why don't you come and visit me, my mom and dad, my sister and my grandmother, and our dog, Fluffy? We have an extra room in the attic and the Secret Service can sleep in our barn.

Ethan N., AGE 8
Syracuse, NY

Dear President Bush,

I would like to visit you in the White House when I am not too busy.

Love,
Cynthia G., AGE **8**
Carlsbad, NM

Dear President,

I don't think you should let girls go in the army. Girls are a pain and they cry a lot.

Yours truly,
Jay B., AGE **7**
Denver, CO

Dear President Bush,

If I were president I would pick Mrs. Clinton to be my vice president.

She is very smart and she could always ask President Clinton to help you.

Heather L., AGE **9**
Farmington, MS

Dear President Bush,

Please send me a list of all the enemies of our country.

My Boy Scout troop wants to watch out for them.

Christopher P., AGE **8**
Chicago, IL

Dear Mr. President,

If I were president I would do something right away about clean air.

Everybody in my house is always sneezing and coughing.

Sandy L., AGE 9
Los Angeles, CA

Dear Mr. President,

My mom and dad fight all the time. Could you help?

Maybe you could put them both in the army so they could fight with the enemy—not each other.

Samuel J., AGE 9
Dublin, GA

Dear President Bush,

I think you should listen to kids.

Not all kids are stupid like my cousin Mark.

Your friend,
Abby J., AGE 7
Dallas, TX

Dear President Bush,

Do you like to take naps? My dad likes to take naps but he's grouchy if we wake him up. It's hard to play quiet. My little brother is pretty noisy.

Who is in charge of the White House if you take naps? Are you grouchy too when you wake up?

Heather I., AGE 9
Macon, GA

To the President,

Please call me at 677-4288.

I need your help with my homework.

Thank you,
Kaitlyn G., AGE 8
Tallmadge, OH

P.S. I promise I will vote for you when I'm old enough to vote.

Dear President Bush,

What are you going to do for old people? Someday you will be old too.

Love,
Linda J., AGE 9
Chadron, NE

Dear Sir,

I think you should move the White House close to Disneyland.

Then more people will want to visit the White House.

Your citizen,
Ralph S., AGE 8
Hudson, OH

Dear President Bush,

If I were president we would have only one day of school a week.

Then we could watch more TV and we could learn more.

Logan B., AGE 7
Fresno, CA

Dear Mr. President,

Call me if you need any help.

I am very smart and my father is a Republican and my mother is a Democrat and my big sister doesn't vote because she only likes boys.

Your friend,
Alan M., AGE 10
Abilene, TX

Dear Mr. President,

Were you ever president of your class in school?

I am president of my class so maybe I can be president of the country if I don't flunk geography. Sometimes I get mixed up when I look at the map. Especially with China and Japan and India.

Your friend,
Isabella P., AGE 8
Salinas, CA

Dear President Bush,

Were you ever spanked when you were a kid?

I bet your parents would never have spanked you if they knew you were going to be president.

Nicholas M., AGE **8**
Springfield, MO

Dear President Bush,

There are too many poor people in Chicago. Please send them some money.

Taylor B., AGE **8**
Chicago, IL

Dear President Bush,

I read that there are 32 bathrooms in the White House.

I would like to come to the White House someday and use a bathroom.

Love,
Mandy R., AGE **9**
New Haven, CT

Dear Mr. President,

Why do you have to be 16 to drive a car?

I am 7 and I can ride a bike. I will have to wait a long time until I am old enough to drive a car.

Kyle M., AGE 7
Austin, TX

Dear President Bush,

Did you ever see any of President Reagan's movies?

Did you think he was a good actor?

I thought he was the best actor that ever became president.

Christina C., AGE 9
Brunswick, ME

Dear President Bush,

I would like to be the first woman president but first I want to be Miss America.

Love,
Samantha G., AGE 8
Purdue, IN

Dear Mr. President,

Does the president get free food at the White House?

I would like to have lunch at the White House but I will bring my own peanut butter sandwiches for you and me and the First Lady.

Sydney C., AGE 7
Riverside, CA

Dear Mr. Bush,

I think the flowers in the rose garden at the White House are beautiful.

Could I come to the White House and pick a bunch of flowers to give my mother on Mother's Day?

I think my mother voted for you.

Elizabeth D., AGE 9
Baltimore, MD

Dear President Bush,

What size shoes do you wear?

My grandfather died last month and he left a lot of shoes and my brother and I would like to send you and the vice president a pair of shoes.

Do you like brown shoes or black shoes?

We will shine the shoes before we send them to you.

Joey P.

Age 8

Erie, PA

Dear President Bush,

Please send my math teacher to the moon before our next test.

> Thank you,
> *Alyssa F.,* AGE 9
> Long Beach, CA

Dear President Bush,

If I were president everybody in the country would be happy because there would be no taxes and there would be free TV and cookies.

> *Claire A.,* AGE 9
> Washington, DC

Dear President Bush,

Did your mother know you would be president when you were born?

When I was born my mother wanted me to be a doctor because doctors make all the money, after baseball players.

> *Andrew C.,* AGE 8
> Westport, CT

P.S. I play shortstop.

Dear Mr. President,

I would like to read the story of your life.
I am seven so I can't read it if there are big words.

Jeff G., AGE 7
Lancaster, PA

Dear Mr. President,

If I were president I would give the vice president something to do.

The vice president gets a lot of money but he doesn't do much work.

Jordan R., AGE 7
Modesto, CA

Dear President Bush,

Who does the grocery shopping for the White House? Do you or the First Lady or the Secret Service shop?

Do you get your food cheaper than everybody else?

Eric K., AGE 10
Middletown, CT

Dear Mr. President,

Who writes your speeches?

Maybe you should get the writer for the *David Letterman Show* so your speeches will be funny.

People like funny presidents.

Alyssa K., AGE 11
New York, NY

Dear Mr. President,

I would like my cat Felix to come and live with you at the White House. Then Felix would be the First Cat.

Thank you,
Bailey B., AGE 7
Madison, WI

P.S. Felix is a very neat cat and he always uses his litter box.

Dear Mr. President,

Do you have any friends in Congress?

Do you know Mike Wallace?

Please send me a letter so I can show it to my friend Stanton who doesn't think I know anybody important.

Brandon N., AGE 8
Glendale, RI

Dear President Bush,

You made a lot of promises when you were running for president.

I hope you keep your promises especially the promise about fewer taxes.

My mother and father don't like to pay taxes and if they pay fewer taxes I will get more allowance so I can take my girlfriend Anna to the movies.

Gavin H., AGE 10
Des Moines, IA

Dear Mr. President,

We have lots of problems in Iraq.

I hope you can solve the problems in Iraq because everybody in Detroit is worried.

Your friend,
Marsha A., AGE 9
Detroit, MI

Dear President Bush,

Did you know you would win the election?

Did you tell your kids you would win the election or were they surprised like everybody else?

Aaron F., AGE 7
Oakland, CA

Dear Mr. Bush,

I would like to go into the National Guard so I could help our country and get rid of all our enemies like Bruce in my history class.

Nicole B., AGE 9
Wilmington, DE

Dear Mr. President,

America is the best country because we have the best ice cream. Chocolate is my favorite.

Dylan T., AGE 7
Akron, OH

Dear Mr. President,

I knew you would win the election when my best friend Amy said you would lose.

Amy is always wrong.

Julie P., AGE 9
Exeter, RI

Dear President Bush,

Did you want to be a football player when you were a kid?

I want to be a football player, a basketball player, a soccer player or play tennis.

Maybe I can be president if I can't get on the teams.

Connor N., AGE 7
Springfield, IL

Dear President Bush,

I think you should get a snake.

Then you will be the first president who has a snake in the White House except when Congress comes over to visit.

Robert H., AGE **10**
San Antonio, TX

Dear Mr. President,

I think we should bring all the soldiers home from Iraq for Christmas.

Christmas is no fun in Iraq.

Jacob H., AGE 9
Topeka, KS

Dear Mr. President,

In school my teacher said the president of the United States is the smartest man in the country.

My teacher should meet my father.

Hayden C., AGE 10
Willoughby, OH

Dear President Bush,

Did you ever ride a subway in New York?

Don't ride the subway without the Secret Service.

Your friend,
Michelle T., AGE 8
Bronx, NY

Dear Mr. President,

On TV you didn't answer some questions because you said the answer was classified.

Can I classify my answers?

I got in trouble when I admitted I broke something I shouldn't have touched. If I could say the answer is classified, I wouldn't be in trouble.

Martin J., AGE 9
Philadelphia, PA

Dear Mr. Bush,

Where did you meet the First Lady? How old were you?

Did you kiss her on your first date?

I have a girlfriend, but I'm afraid to kiss her until I am older or president or a baseball player.

Jeremy F., AGE 7
Gallup, NM

Dear President Bush,

What is your e-mail address? Do you read your e-mail?

I would write to you a lot more but I don't have money for stamps. You can e-mail me back so you can save money too.

Hunter J., AGE 9
Alexandria, VA

Dear Mr. President,

Was the First Lady your girlfriend when you were a kid? Amy is my girlfriend and if I am the president she will be the First Lady.

Mason J., AGE 11
Lansing, MI

Dear Mr. President,

Do you have to be rich to run for president? I hope not because all I have is 69 cents.

Anthony C., AGE 7
Bronx, NY

Dear President Bush,

What was your best subject in school?

My best subject in school is lunch, especially on pizza days.

Zachary C., AGE 8
Anniston, AL

Dear Mr. Bush,

I want to know what you are going to do for the nine-year-old kids in America.

I will be nine years old next week.

Matthew J., AGE ALMOST 9
Yuma, AZ

Dear Mr. President,

Is it true you have your very own bathroom on Air Force One?

I would like to fly on Air Force One so I can go to the bathroom in the sky.

Jimmy V., AGE 7
Providence, RI

Dear Mr. President,

If I were president I would let kids stay home from school on their birthdays.

My birthday is January 22.

Chuck M., AGE 8
Jefferson City, TN

Dear Mr. Bush,

Were you ever a Boy Scout?

I am a Cub Scout and then someday I hope to be a Boy Scout and then I will decide if I want to be president.

Luke O., AGE 8
Amarillo, TX

Dear President Bush,

Can you watch any TV shows that you want to?

My mom won't let me watch reality TV shows after she saw me collecting worms.

Anthony B., AGE 10
Detroit, MI

Dear President Bush,

Do you like to travel?

It must be great to be president because you can travel for free. What is your favorite country?

I think I would like the North Pole because I like polar bears.

Gabrielle W., AGE 8
Pittsburgh, PA

Dear President Bush,

I think your wife is beautiful.

She should have her own TV show.

She would make a lot of money because TV stars make more money than First Ladies.

Kyra L., AGE 9
Eureka, CA

Dear President Bush,

My dog Baxter died. He was a really brave dog.

Could he be buried in Arlington cemetery where brave soldiers and presidents are buried?

Angela B., AGE 9
Bethesda, MD

Dear Mr. President,

I would like to be president someday so I could get to meet a lot of famous people like Johnny Depp.

Mackenzie G., AGE 10
Lake Placid, NY

Dear President Bush,

My grandpa said President Nixon said he was not a crook.

Does that mean other presidents were crooks?

Milton H., AGE 8
El Paso, TX

Dear Mr. President,

Was President Clinton the smartest president we ever had?

My teacher, Mrs. Curtis, said the smartest president was FDR and after FDR it was JFK.

I still think that President Clinton was the smartest because he wrote a very long book. You have to be very smart to write a book with so many words.

Kristin S.

Age 11

Phoenix, AZ

Dear President Bush,

How come you have a secretary of state, a secretary of defense, a treasury secretary, but you don't have a kids' secretary?

Even if kids can't vote, they have rights too.

Chase M., AGE 8
Bangor, ME

Dear Mr. Bush,

I would like to be the first lady president.

I am very smart and I get good grades and my mom says I am very neat so I won't mess up the White House.

Abigail N., AGE 9
Roanoke, VA

P.S. My big brother is a slob.

Dear President Bush,

Is it safe to fly on a plane?

My big brother says that the only thing that is safe is a bike.

Cameron A., AGE 8
Little Rock, AR

Dear President Bush,

My Uncle Mario is a barber.

He is the best barber in Buffalo, New York.

He would like to come to the White House to give you a haircut. He will only charge you 50 cents because you are the president and he said it will be good for his business.

Albert B., AGE 8
Buffalo, NY

Dear President Bush,

What do you eat for breakfast?

I have orange juice and cereal with fruit and milk.

Mom says that is a very good breakfast because it is good for you.

I would like to have a candy bar.

Skippy K., AGE 7
Cedar City, UT

Dear President Bush,

Does anybody call you by your first name or does everybody call you Mr. President?

You can call me by my first name. It is Nancy.

Nancy R., AGE 9
Cody, WY

Dear Mr. President,

Why don't the French people like the United States?

My parents aren't going to eat in any more French restaurants.

They are still going to eat Chinese food.

Emily B., AGE 8
Philadelphia, PA

Dear Sir,

I like to watch your speeches on TV even if I don't understand what you are saying.

Maybe next time you could make a special speech for kids.

Samuel J., AGE 8
Andover, MA

Dear President Bush,

My mother wrote this letter for me because I can't write yet. Someday I will be able to write and then I will be able to vote and I will vote for you.

Please write back because I can read even if I can't write.

Sydney J., AGE 5
Louisville, KY

Dear President Bush,

You are in good shape. Do you exercise every day?

My dad can do eight pushups and he uses the treadmill every day.

If you need him to help you to exercise you can call us on the phone.

Mark G., AGE 11
Flagstaff, AZ

Dear Mr. President,

Does the White House have a swimming pool?

Do you need a lifeguard? I took the Jr. Life Guard class and passed the test to be a Jr. Life Guard. Let me know if you need me.

Allison K., AGE 12
Santa Barbara, CA

Dear Mr. President,

Who is the boss in the White House?

You or the First Lady? My mom is the boss in our house.

Carl S., AGE 9
Milwaukee, WI

Dear Mr. Bush,

Are the Russians our friends now? Do you think we should trust them?

My grandfather was a soldier in World War II and he doesn't think we should trust Russians even if they swear on the Bible.

William P., AGE 8
Salt Lake City, UT

Dear President Bush,

I think ex-Mayor Giuliani would be a great president when you become ex-president.

You should invite him to the White House so he can learn the job.

Matthew W., AGE 8
Brooklyn, NY

Dear Mr. President,

If you need any help in the White House you can call me collect after 6:00 p.m.

Faith L., AGE **8**
Denver, CO

Dear President Bush,

Do you have a dog?

Who has to walk the dog in the rain, you or the First Lady?

Melissa T., AGE **9**
Philadelphia, PA

Dear Mr. Bush,

If I were president I would have a lady as secretary of the army and secretary of state and vice president.

Women are very smart and men are not so smart.

That is why we have so much fighting in the world.

Hailey B., AGE **9**
Palm Springs, CA

Dear President Bush,

Do you ever tell jokes?

I collect jokes and I would like to have a joke from you because I don't have any jokes from a president.

Your friend,
Kyle H., AGE 8
Phoenix, AZ

P.S. If you don't have any jokes you could ask the vice president.

Dear Mr. President,

My history teacher told us the White House is very old.

Did George Washington live in the same White House?

Maybe you should move to a new White House before the old White House falls down.

Austin G., AGE 10
Saginaw, MI

Dear President Bush,

My father is a plumber. He says that a plumber works very hard.

Could you help my father get a job where he doesn't have to work so hard?

It's no fun when your father doesn't do anything but fall asleep watching TV when he comes home.

Brian C., AGE 9
Burlington, VT

Dear President Bush,

Do you have any brothers or sisters?

I'm the only kid in my family so I have to do the dishes and take out the garbage all the time. I think we ought to adopt another kid.

Do you know where we could get one?

Also can you adopt kids old enough to help with jobs around the house? Adopting a baby would be no good.

Bobbie M., AGE 8
Dallas, TX

Dear President Bush,

I hope you get a good job when you are the ex-president.

Maybe you could work at McDonald's.

Anna P., AGE 7
Savannah, GA

Dear Mr. President,

Do you hate Congress?

My dad said you and Congress don't get along very good.

Jimmy O., AGE 7
Hicksville, NY

Hi Mr. President,

I would like to come to the White House to shake your hand because I have never shaken hands with a president before.

I will wash my hands before we shake.

Thank you,
Wendy W., AGE 9
Albuquerque, NM

Dear Mr. President,

My father likes you a lot except when he has to pay his taxes.

Brooke D., AGE **9**
Reston, VA

Dear President Bush,

I like "The Star Spangled Banner" but I think we should get a new national anthem that is easier to sing.

Nobody can remember the words and the song is hard to sing.

Grace D., AGE **10**
Asheville, NC

Dear President Bush,

Could you please name a spaceship for me?

I want to be the first boy in my class that goes to the moon.

Thank you,
Evan Y., AGE **10**
Roswell, NM

Dear President Bush,

My grandmother is very sick.

She needs somebody to take care of her but we don't have enough money to get somebody.

Could my dad borrow the money from the White House? My dad is a very hard worker and I know he will pay you back someday.

Emma N., AGE 9
Greenville, MI

Dear Mr. President,

Did any presidents' kids ever have a tree house? Were they allowed to have sleepovers?

Did the Secret Service guard it?

I want to have a tree house but my mom thinks I'll fall and get hurt. Please write and say they are safe. My mom voted for you, so she'll believe you.

Jenna L., AGE 8
Baltimore, MD

Dear Mr. President,
My girlfriend Alyssa is a Republican and I am a Democrat. Someday we may get married.
Can a Democrat marry a Republican and be happy?
I am 12 and my girlfriend is 11. We would like your answer before we are 18.

Thank you,
Ryan C.
Age 12
Philadelphia, PA

Dear Mr. President,

I wish I was president so I could have the Secret Service and the FBI take care of the big kids who are always punching me.

Hunter L., AGE 7
Knoxville, TN

Dear Mr. President,

I wrote down everything you promised during the election. I hope you keep your word.

I will write you again if you don't keep your word.

Natalie W., AGE 12
Rochester, NY

Dear President Bush,

My father said that when you become an ex-president you will get a million dollars a speech.

What do you say that is worth a million dollars?

I would like you to speak to our chess club but we can only pay you $10.00.

Stacy, AGE 11
Tampa, FL

Dear Mr. President,

Who was the best president that ever lived? Is it you?

Kimberly B., AGE 9
Boise, ID

Dear Mr. President,

I think you should read the speeches of Abraham Lincoln. Then maybe people won't fall asleep when they hear you talk.

Jeremy J., AGE 10
Sidney, NE

Dear Mr. President,

I would like your autograph so I can trade it for 50 cents.

I can send you 10 cents for your autograph.

Benjamin G., AGE 7
Pierre, SD

Dear President Bush,

I would like to come to the White House so you can help me with my homework.

My big brother tries to help me with my homework because my dad said he had to, but he is a big dope and I know you are smart or you wouldn't be president.

Thank you,
Ashley Y., AGE 7
Missoula, MT

Dear Mr. President,

Where do you buy your clothes?

My mom says it looks like you get them from a secondhand store or a store that sells cheap clothes.

You should look at pictures of President Kennedy. He was always well dressed and that is why everybody likes him. Nobody likes a president who doesn't dress sharp.

Abigail H., AGE 13
Denver, CO

Dear Mr. President,

I am proud to be an American and I will do anything for my country except eat cereal for breakfast every day.

Could you please write my mom and tell her I can be a good American without eating cereal? I like peanut butter and jelly.

Hunter C., AGE 11
San Jose, CA

Dear President Bush,

What is your favorite TV program? Can you watch TV a lot?

My mom only lets me watch TV one hour a day. Does the First Lady let you watch when you want to?

Are you allowed to watch cartoons? I think you would have more fun if you watched cartoons instead of the news.

Adam Y., AGE 9
Augusta, GA

Dear President Bush,
   The funniest president was President Ronald Reagan.
   You should use some of his jokes. Your jokes aren't so good.

Chase F., AGE **8**
Pittsburgh, PA

Dear President Bush,
   I think you should answer all the letters you receive from every American even if they didn't vote for you.

Nicole T., AGE **9**
Tulsa, OK

Dear Mr. President,
   How long have you been married?
   Do you and the First Lady ever fight?
   My mom and dad have been married for 20 years and they fight all the time except when they are sleeping.

Kayla G., AGE **13**
Billings, MT

Dear President Bush,

I think the best thing about being president is that nobody can tell you what to do.

When you are a kid everybody tells you what to do, especially your big sister.

Logan N., AGE 7
Orlando, FL

Dear President Bush,

Does the First Lady cook dinner for you at the White House?

Is she a good cook like my mom?

Lauren M., AGE 10
Providence, RI

Dear President Bush,

Our bowling club would like to invite you to bowl with us on Tuesdays after school. I hope you can come.

We promise to let you win.

Ella P., AGE 9
Rapid City, SD

Dear President Bush,
    Do you ever play tricks on the vice president?
                        Eric A., AGE 7
                        Hartford, CT

Dear Mr. President,

I read in the newspaper that you have your own barber in the White House.

I would like to come to the White House for a haircut. I can pay 25 cents.

Adam D., AGE 7
Richmond, VA

★

Dear Mr. President,

Have you ever been to Boston? Boston is a great city. Harvard is in Boston so we have a lot of smart people.

Jacob H., AGE 10
Boston, MA

★

Dear President Bush,

Do you get angry when you read what they say about you in the newspapers?

My father said that if he was president he would never read another newspaper, but he gets mad at everything, even the weather reports on TV.

Annie P., AGE 9
Asheville, NC

Dear President Bush,
    What do you do for fun?
    Do you watch Congress on TV?
                                    Jennifer V., AGE 8
                                    Helena, MT

Dear Mr. President,
    I am the president of my class.
    I would like to run for reelection but I made a lot of campaign promises that I didn't keep. What should I do?
    My mom said you would know.
                                    Andrew L., AGE 11
                                    Reno, NV

Dear Mr. President,
    Did you ever play baseball when you were a kid?
    Were you a pitcher or did you just sell popcorn and hot dogs?
                                    Caleb T., AGE 8
                                    Laredo, TX

Dear Mr. President,

Did you want to be president of the country when you were nine?

I am nine and I don't know if I want to be president when I grow up or coach of the L.A. Lakers.

If you are not too busy could you please write to me and give me your opinion?

Thank you,
Steve G., AGE 9
Los Angeles, CA

Dear President Bush,

My friend Margie and me would like to put together a book of all the funny things you have ever said.

So far we only have half a page.

Could you send us some of the funny things you have said so that we can have a full page?

Thank you,
Emma T., AGE 10
Asheville, NC

Dear Mr. President,

I think you won the election because you don't use too many big words in your speeches.

Daniel K., AGE **8**
Fort Wayne, IN

Dear President Bush,

They charge too much money for peanut butter sandwiches in my school lunchroom.

Could you send us free peanut butter sandwiches? We promise to vote for you when we are 18.

Mason C., AGE 7
Lexington, KY

Dear President Bush,

Do you have to make your own bed or does the First Lady make your bed?

I have to make my own bed because the only first lady we have in our house is my mom and she doesn't make kids' beds.

William D., AGE **8**
Albuquerque, NM

Dear President Bush,

I like to hear you talk on TV but I would rather watch *The Simpsons*.

Kevin D., AGE 8
Knoxville, TN

Dear President Bush,

My friend Stewart is always fighting with other kids in school. Nobody wants to fight with him because he is very strong.

I think you should send Stewart to the marines.

Jackson J., AGE 9
Grand Rapids, MI

Dear Mr. President,

Do you think we will have a war with China?

I hope not because me and my mom and dad like Chinese food a lot but not my brother. He only likes hot dogs or bologna sandwiches.

Ryan B., AGE 11
Pittsburgh, PA

Dear Mr. President,

My big sister said Homeland Security would work better if people used dogs for their home security. Dogs are smart and brave and good at watching homes and there are a lot of dogs that need homes too.

Sarah M.
Age 9
New York, NY

Dear President Bush,

Do you have a lot of friends?

I am president of my class at school and I have a lot of friends except for Freddy.

Freddy wanted to be president of his class but nobody voted for him. Not even his twin sister.

She voted for me.

Danny J., AGE 9
Shreveport, LA

Dear Mr. President,

I saw on TV that they have White House tours.

Does that mean that you have to clean your room before people get there?

I always have to clean my room when we have company, even if it's not company for me.

I keep my half of the room neat but my brother is really messy and I have to help him.

Justin W., AGE 8
Asheville, NC

Dear President Bush,

   I would like an autographed picture. I already have one from Britney Spears.

Alexis B., AGE 9
Colorado Springs, CO

Dear President Bush,

   I wish my father was president so I could get all the kids in my class to call me "sir" instead of "jerk."

Tony P., AGE 7
Detroit, MI

Dear Mr. President,

   Is Russia our enemy or are they our friends now?

   I hope they are friends because my new girlfriend is from Russia.

   She has been in this country for six months and she likes it very much except for the pizza.

Kevin D. , AGE 10
Brooklyn, NY

Dear President Bush,

I am glad you won the election because you were the best looking.

Angela K., AGE 7
Charleston, WV

Dear President Bush,

I hope our country never has another war like the war in Iraq.

Nobody likes war except stupid people. My best friend's uncle is in Iraq.

Cynthia V., AGE 10
Detroit, MI

Dear Mr. President,

How many hours a day does the president work? How many hours a day does the vice president work?

Please write and tell me so I can decide if I want to be president or vice president.

Thank you,
George T., AGE 11
Lubbock, TX

Dear Mr. President,

Who is smarter? The Republicans or the Democrats?

My teacher says they are all the same but my father thinks Republicans are smarter. My mom says she isn't sure.

She thinks they are both a little dopey.

Lauren H., AGE 9
Indianapolis, IN

Dear Mr. President,

Someday if we have a woman president we will need more closets in the White House so the president will have room for all her clothes.

My mom has three closets and my sister has two closets and my dad and my brother and I have to share closets.

Michael P., AGE 8
San Diego, CA

Dear President Bush,

I saw on TV everybody was looking for some big weapons in Iraq. I find lots of lost things under my bed.

Maybe they should look under some beds in Iraq.

Jonathan G., AGE 10
Boston, MA

Dear Mr. President,

Did you ever meet President Clinton?

He was my favorite president except for President Kennedy.

Alexandra H., AGE 8
Bethesda, MD

Dear President Bush,

I want to be an FBI agent when I grow up.

If I can't be an FBI agent I would like to be a spy for America.

Thank you for your help,
Mason D., AGE 9
St. Paul, MN

Dear President Bush,

Could you make a law that teachers can't yell when you don't do your homework?

My teacher always yells even if there is only one kid in the class that didn't do his homework.

Most of the time that kid is me.

Bobbie Y., AGE 10
Charlotte, NC

Dear President Bush,

If I were president I would send all the girls in my class to the North Pole.

Hunter D., AGE 8
Fargo, ND

Dear Mr. Bush,

What do they do in Congress?
My father told me they don't do much but talk.

Chloe D., AGE 9
Alexandria, VA

Dear President Bush,

Do you have your own TV set in the White House?

There are five kids in our family and we only have one TV set. We are always fighting about what to watch on TV but my big brother always wins.

Cameron H., AGE 7
Lawton, OK

Dear President Bush,

Does the First Lady make you eat all your vegetables?

My mom even makes me eat cauliflower and green beans.

If you made a law that some vegetables were illegal or un-American, I bet lots of kids would vote for you when they were old enough.

Jeremy A., AGE 8
Baltimore, MD

Dear President Bush,

I saw on TV that you were riding on a bus to talk to voters.

Is your airplane in the garage being fixed? My mom's car is in the garage a lot for fixing. My dad said she needs a new car. Maybe you need to buy a new airplane.

Tyler T., AGE 9
Brooklyn, NY

Dear President Bush,

The people next door have a dog that barks all the time.

Please send the FBI.

Thank you,
Jason P., AGE 7
Aspen, CO

Dear Mr. President,

Do you tell the First Lady what you did in your office all day?

My dad doesn't tell my mom what he does at the office because my mom thinks it is boring.

Brianna E., AGE 10
Santa Fe, CA

Dear President Bush,

I would rather be vice president because all the vice president has to do all day is to worry that the president doesn't get sick because then he would have to go to work.

Adam C., AGE 10
Eau Claire, WI

Dear President Bush,

Were you ever in the army? What did you do in the army?

Did you tell everybody what to do like when you are president?

Jack S., AGE **8**
Omaha, NE

Dear Mr. President,

Someday when there is a woman president I would like to be the assistant to the president.

I would be a good assistant because I am very neat and I spell good.

Lauren D., AGE **10**
Norfolk, VA

Dear President Bush,

If we have another war in Iraq I would like to send my big brother. How old does he have to be?

Caleb J., AGE **8**
Brownsville, TX

Dear Mr. President,

Do you have to be pretty to be the First Lady?

My best friend Stacy wants to be the First Lady but she is ugly—but she is smart and very nice.

Do you think she can still be First Lady?

Julia D., AGE 10
Billings, MT

Dear Mr. President,

My Uncle Alex was in the Vietnam War and he says war is really bad.

If people want to fight, instead of shooting bullets they should use those paint guns that shoot paint balls. We did that at camp and it's a lot of fun and nobody is hurt when the game is over. The paint washes off pretty good.

Tommy B., AGE 9
Syracuse, NY

Dear Mr. Bush,

My grandmother is 98 years old.
I think she even voted for President Lincoln.

Amanda P., AGE 8
Myrtle Beach, SC

Dear President Bush,

What do you do when you are in the Oval Office?

Do you call a lot of famous people around the world? Do you have to pay for your own phone calls?

Gabrielle D., AGE 9
Tulsa, OK

Dear President Bush,

Are you or the vice president in charge of garbage?

We need more garbage men in Spokane. The sidewalks and streets are always dirty except in front of my house because my mom is the cleanest mom in Spokane and she sweeps the sidewalk every day.

Luke D., AGE 8
Spokane, WA

Dear President Bush,

I would like to be the first lady president.

I would be a great president because I am very neat and I know how to make my own bed so that our country would save money because I wouldn't need an FBI agent to make my bed every morning.

Amanda A.
Age 9
Cheyenne, WY

Dear Mr. President,
 I don't think it's safe in Brooklyn anymore.
Please send the marines.
Andy B., AGE 7
Brooklyn, NY

Dear Mr. President,
 What does the vice president do when you are sleeping?
 Is that when he becomes the president?
Megan H., AGE 9
Redding, CA

Dear President Bush,
 I don't know if I want to be president of the country when I grow up because they always say bad things about you on TV and in the newspapers.
Connor T., AGE 12
Montgomery, AL

Dear Mr. President,

Is your dog allowed to sleep on your bed?

My mom said my dog can sleep with me only if he gets more baths. Rascal hates to get a bath and he jumps out of the bathtub and gets the bathroom all wet.

Do you have to give your dog a bath or does the Secret Service do that? If they do, you are very lucky.

Ryan G., AGE 9
Albany, NY

Dear President Bush,

I've been practicing piano for two years and I hate it and I am awful. My mom said President Nixon played piano. Did you have to play piano because President Nixon did?

I think two years of being a bad player is enough.

Please write to my mom and tell her. She likes you most of the time.

Melissa E., AGE 10
Shaker Heights, OH

Dear President Bush,

    Do you know Peter Jennings?

    He talks a lot about you on TV.

Jacob L., AGE **10**

Indianapolis, IN

Dear Mr. President,

    My grandmother says everybody should eat a banana a day.

    I am sending you five bananas.

Stephanie T., AGE **8**

Biloxi, MS

Dear Mr. President,

    Did you do your homework every day when you were a kid like me?

    I hope not because I would like to be president someday and I hate to do homework.

Adam T., AGE **8**

Omaha, NE

Dear Mr. President,

Do presidents go to heaven when they die?
Do they have to be Republicans or Democrats?

Angela S., AGE 7
Scranton, PA

Dear Mr. Bush,

There are too many girls and dogs on my block.
Please help me.

Thank you,
Matthew D., AGE 7
Buffalo, NY

Dear President Bush,

I wish I had known President Kennedy. He was
the handsomest president.

He was a lot more handsome than Abraham
Lincoln.

Taylor K., AGE 9
Tulsa, OK

Dear Mr. President,

Did you or the First Lady ever want to paint the White House a different color?

My mom loves to decorate and I bet she could help you if you ask her.

If the White House gets painted blue or yellow would people have to call it the Blue House or the Yellow House?

Amy D., AGE **8**
Wilmington, DE

Dear President Bush,

Do presidents get report cards?

I got good grades on my last report card so I got to go to the movies and buy popcorn.

If you got report cards then Congress couldn't complain about you on TV so much. They would have to wait until report card time.

Kevin G., AGE **8**
Dallas, TX

Dear Mr. President,

Was President Clinton the best president or just the best talker?

Adrienne F., AGE 10
Little Rock, AR

Dear Mr. President,

You are lucky because the president gets to throw out the first pitch at the World Series and you don't even have to buy a ticket to the game.

Justin A., AGE 10
Los Angeles, CA

Dear Mr. President,

What is the best thing about being president?

My friend Paul says that the best thing about being president is that you don't have to pay for lunch.

It costs $1.25 for lunch at my school and the food isn't worth 2¢.

Morris E., AGE 8
Jacksonville, FL

Dear Mr. President,

Did you ever go to Disneyland on vacation?

Do you have to take the Secret Service with you? They don't look like they are much fun to be with.

Daniel P., AGE **8**
Huntington, IN

Dear President Bush,

Could you please call me on the telephone? Nobody ever calls me except wrong numbers.

Ethan M., AGE 9
Burlington, VT

Dear President Bush,

I live in the country and I would like you to come visit our farm so I can show you how to milk a cow.

Danny T., AGE 9
Murrysville, PA

Dear Mr. President,

My father says if you are president and you make a mistake you can always blame it on the vice president.

If the vice president makes a mistake who can he blame it on?

Nicolas G., AGE 7
Cheyenne, WY

Dear Mr. President,

My father can't sleep too good at night because of all the noise in New York.

Can't you do something about the noise in New York?

When he doesn't get enough sleep he is grouchy about everything. Please help.

Peter S., AGE 8
Brooklyn, NY

Dear Mr. President,

Do you ever yell at the First Lady?

Does the First Lady ever yell at you?

My dad never yells at my mom but my mom yells at everybody except the dog. I think she likes the dog best.

Mia G., AGE 9
Bakersfield, CA

Dear Mr. President,

Did you write a letter to the president when you were little?

Our social studies class all had to write letters to our congressman to say we need more money for schools. I hope he listens because my dad said a good education is very important and he's smart.

Ethan F., AGE **10**
Orlando, FL

Dear President Bush,

I like your jokes.

My mother likes your jokes.

My father likes your jokes.

My grandfather doesn't laugh at your jokes because he is deaf.

William G., AGE **8**
Charlotte, NC

Dear President Bush,

How much money does the vice president make? If it is more than $2.00 a week he is getting too much.

Adam T., AGE 7
Scranton, PA

Dear Mr. Bush,

It must be great to have your own airplane. All I have is an old bike that I got from my big brother.

Tommy T., AGE 8
Columbus, OH

Dear Mr. President,

Is the First Lady smarter than you? My mom is smarter than my dad but she lets him think he is smarter than she is. Does the First Lady do that too?

Hannah L., AGE 9
Saginaw, MI

Dear President Bush,

How old do you have to be, to be a spy for the CIA?

I am twelve and I think I would be a good spy because I spy on my big sister all the time.

Gary G., AGE 12
Portland, OR

Dear Mr. President,

Sometimes the newspapers write bad things about you.

Maybe you should only read the comics in the papers so you won't get mad.

Carl J., AGE 8
Baltimore, MD

Dear Mr. Bush,

Did you spank your kids when they were little? I hope the answer is no.

Please write my mom and dad and tell them you don't think spanking is good for American kids.

Teresa A., AGE 8
St. Louis, MO

Dear President Bush,

I liked all the speeches at the convention except the speeches I couldn't understand which were most of them.

Uncle Barney said he didn't understand them either but he thought it didn't matter because he said they were all lying. My mom got mad and told him to go home.

Everybody liked all the balloons at the convention.

Stacy P.
Age 9
Austin, TX

Dear President Bush,

Did you know President Reagan?

He was my father's favorite president. He thought President Reagan was very funny.

He told me some of President Reagan's jokes, but I didn't understand them.

Steve M., AGE 8
Creston, IA

Dear Mr. President,

I think you are a good-looking president. You are better looking than George Washington.

Richard U., AGE 9
Providence, RI

Dear President Bush,

Is God a Democrat or a Republican?
Please write and tell me.

Gail T., AGE 8
Lawrenceburg, KY

P.S. I hope he is a Republican like my dad.

Dear President Bush,

Could you please pass a law that says every kid can get a free bike?

I need a new bike but my mom and dad said they can't buy me one because they have to pay too much in taxes.

Christopher M., AGE 7
Rochester, NY

Dear Mr. President,

I think I would be a great Secret Service agent because I know how to protect people.

My little brother is five and nobody hurts him when I am around.

Andy T., AGE 8
Columbus, OH

Dear President Bush,

Is England our best friend in the world?

I like England but I also like Ireland because my father is Irish and he knows a lot of Irish songs.

Shawn O., AGE 7
Boston, MA

Dear President Bush,

Did you read ex-President Clinton's book?

I want to read it but my mother says the book is too long and costs too much money.

I hope when you write a book it is only 20 pages long and it is cheap to buy.

Samuel E., AGE 9
Davenport, IA

Dear Mr. President,

Do you get mad at the reporters asking questions all the time?

A lot of them talk at the same time. My teacher makes us raise our hands and wait till she calls our name before we can talk.

Maybe you should tell the reporters to raise their hands and wait until you call on them before they can talk.

Your friend,
Samantha J., AGE 8
Bethesda, MD

Dear President Bush,

I would like to take a picture with you so I can put the picture on the wall in my room next to my picture of Madonna.

Mallory P., AGE 8
Hartford, CT

Dear Mr. President,

Did you know that you wanted to be president when you were a kid?

I am nine years old and I don't know what I want to be except I don't want to be vice president because nobody pays attention to the vice president.

Jeremy R., AGE 9
Mobile, AL

Dear Mr. President,

My mom told me that Mr. Kerry saved their hamster from drowning once.

Is that something you do a lot as president? Save small animals from drowning?

Megan B., AGE 7
Wichita, KS

Dear President Bush,

What will you do when you become the ex-president?

Maybe you could get your own TV program like David Letterman or Oprah.

Your friend,
Heather N., AGE 9
Glendale, RI

Dear President Bush,

Please do something about the food in our school.

Nobody likes to eat in the lunchroom, not even Stewart and he eats anything.

Luke N., AGE 8
Chicago, IL

Dear Mr. President,

I thought you were great at the convention but I couldn't watch all of it because my mom and dad like *Seinfeld* better.

They said he was funnier.

Julia H., AGE 10
Milwaukee, WI

Dear President Bush,

I would like to be the first kid to go into space.

I am very brave but I will bring my teddy bear with me.

Stephen E., AGE 7
Council Bluffs, IA

Dear Mr. President,

We saw on TV that the 9/11 group didn't trust the Central Intelligence Company.

Maybe you should ask that guy from the *Jeopardy* program, Mr. Jennings, to work on our country's intelligence. My mom and dad think he is very smart.

Margaret D., AGE 10
Roanoke, VA

Dear Mr. Bush,

Do you and the First Lady like to get e-mail?

My big brother said you didn't even know how to turn on a computer. Tommy thinks he's smarter than almost everybody.

Please write and let me know if you need any help with your computer and send me your e-mail address.

Your friend,
Ashley J., AGE 8
Omaha, NE

Dear Mr. President,

What will you do when you become the ex-president?

My father is retired and he drives my mother crazy.

Jeff G., AGE **8**
Atlanta, GA

Dear President Bush,

Did you have a cell phone when you were a boy? My mom won't let me have one. My dad says I can.

Who wins the fights in the White House? You or the First Lady?

Susie F., AGE **8**
Boston, MA

Dear President Bush,

I think you are a great president.

Could you please pass a law that everybody who voted for you doesn't have to do homework?

I didn't vote for you because I am too young to vote, but I would have, so does that count?

Bruce K., AGE **9**
Glendale, RI

Dear Mr. President,

I drew a picture of you. I hope you like it.

You can hang it in the White House next to the picture of Abraham Lincoln.

Taylor G., AGE 8
Bangor, ME

Dear President Bush,

My favorite president was President Reagan.

My number two favorite president was President Truman. I hope someday you are my favorite president but so far you are number 36.

Jacob T., AGE 9
Eugene, OR

Dear President Bush,

I don't think we should fight any more wars. Too many people get killed in war.

We should try and talk to our enemies and maybe invite them to the White House for dinner.

Paige E., AGE 12
Scottsbluff, NE